THE PROCESS

CHANTELLE SMITH

ISBN: 978-1-7344782-0-4

Published by:
TAJ Publishing LLC

Edited by:
Spirit of Excellence Writing & Editing Services, LLC
www.TakeUpThySword.com

This book is dedicated to God, my children Taylar, AJ, and Jarimiah, my dad Alvin Sr., my mom Wanda, and my brother Alvin, Jr. I love you all dearly and pray and thank God for you every day. I pray this book blesses, sheds light, inspires, and encourages you all. And to every person who has been through a process in life, this is for you.

Preface

I'm at a loss for words right now. When you think you have something great, seemingly, the enemy snatches it away from you through some form or matter and you find yourself relentless to finish what once had so much enthusiasm and motivation behind it. Looking up, it's now six months later and what should've taken only a few months to accomplish now gets you ticked enough to just put it on the back burner for a straight season—let alone seasons. Well, that's what happened to me unfortunately. I could say "everything happens for a reason" or "everything in its due time"—which are true statements for some facets of our lives. But the truth remains, some things happen because we have allowed them to happen whether ignorance is to blame or fear. We freely express emotions that sometimes are not in our best interest. Until we become emotionally mature or sound, we cannot expect to experience or respond to circumstances to the best of our abilities *all the time.*

Today, I reach down into the deep wells of every moral fiber of my being and seek to pull up and pull out anything that would stop me from seeing my destiny and purpose fulfilled now. I've received enough prophecies, had a plethora of dreams, seen many visions, talked personally with the Lord, admired all the confirmations, and seen too many doors to sit in the plunder of greatness hoping it would all come to me. We know the infamous scripture, James 2:26, that "faith without works is dead." And yet, I still thought my faith alone would get me to the next place I always desired to be in Christ—in life.

Well, while such faith and deeds are good…it's not all that I had to do. I had to experience *the process.* Have you ever gone through something in life and after you come out on the other side of that experience you realize: "man, if I would've known then what I know now, I would've done some things differently"? I know you've thought or candidly expressed this in some way. We all have. I've come to accept, however, that had it not been for going through the process, much of what I know now would've been nothing but mere knowledge. But knowledge is only powerful when one understands how to apply and use it.

Back in 2014, I had a dream of me driving a vehicle leading up to a friend's house. Instead of driving up to the house and parking the car to get out, I stopped the vehicle about a quarter of a mile away and walked to the door. Well, as I'm walking, I'm holding my stomach—yes, I was pregnant. As I'm holding my stomach walking towards the door, I noticed some activity going on in the sky. There were helicopters or a plane flying in the air as if there was a war going on. It was far away enough for me to hurry to the house for safety. As I walked up to the front of the door, it opened before I could knock. Tiredly, I ask my friend if I could have my baby there at the house.

The dream had other significant things and scenes going on, but what I am privy to share is why I had to walk to the house and didn't just drive up to it, especially considering what was going on in the atmosphere. Well, as I mulled the dream over a bit, even inquired to a few trusted folks about the revelation, I had to walk the process out. It would've been too easy to simply drive up to the house. I had to endure the uncomfortableness of walking up the road eagerly with shallow pants to birth this baby. I had to cultivate my faith during the process placing my trust in God and not in man. Anytime you dream about being in or driving a vehicle, it is symbolic to ministry or a representation of the type of ministry—or a person's ministry whom you know in real life if not your own car—and the color of the car is also symbolic.

I was walking into a new season of my life and God had to let me go through this process. As I walk you through the process of my life experiences, I hope you are encouraged to write or share your own story or testimony. There are a variety of "story" and "self-help" books on the shelves and various platforms today; but let me tell you, your testimony is not just another "story" to tell—it will be meaningful and impactful to those who will read it. It has been part of what has shaped you to be the man or woman you are today, so share it with others. You would be surprised how much your story can help somebody else who needs to know they aren't alone, they aren't that strange or different than anyone else, or who thinks nobody would understand. You'd be surprised.

As I open the curtains to the highs and lows of this portion of my process, my sincere hope is that it places that "hope deferred" (Proverbs 13:12) in the forefront of your mind and propels you to a new faith, a new desire, and a new expected end.

Table of Contents

Introduction

A process is a series of events or steps that get you from where you are to where you should, desire to, or will be over a given time period. Who really wants to be processed, though? Right, nobody! You may want to sing on many platforms with your gift, but to take vocal lessons...yeah, right! Nobody has time for that. You may want to be the go-to celebrity hair stylist but to practice new techniques and take time to learn about the science behind caring for different hair types...well, nobody has time for that either. Just give me my business and let me shine. The grit, sleepless nights, dedication, consistencies, and motivation are just sometimes way too much. I mean, a process can look and quite frankly be nasty.

Think about the exhausting process a woman goes through to give birth. Physiologically, her weight increases, stretch marks become more visible and/or new, the infamous nose stretch and for some, the skin can change colors slightly and become oily. Towards the third trimester of pregnancy, sleeping can become quite uncomfortable trying to find that right position to get adequate rest. The growing baby inside the womb can push against organs that make for some unpleasant facial expressions. While pregnancy is a beautiful thing and can be a joy to experience, the labor can be an unpleasant process. I won't get into all the visuals, so just imagine what I'm talking about. Perhaps you have experienced seeing a baby being born.

How about the process of establishing new faith in your life? What would it take for you to obtain and maintain a new level of faith? What if the storms and trials of your life that you have experienced happened in order to bring you to your expected, God-intended purpose in life? The choices you made yesterday, whether good or bad, have helped push out or birth what was always in you all along.

To the young and emerging adults, stop trying to figure it all out on your own and think milestones need to be completed by a certain time. Just be. Be expressively you while occupying yourself until the greater fulfillment of life is manifested. If you are in your middle ages of life, I encourage you to not consider the time you think you've lost and/or wasted but instead, consider the time you currently have now to make a difference. I encourage you to go through the process so that you can experience life the way God intended you to experience it—in its abundance. If you are reading this and are much older in age, your experiences, wisdom, and presence is as important now to those who love you as it was 30 and 40 years ago…believe that.

Now, let me explain how this book is written so you gain a better understanding as you are reading it; and I pray it truly blesses you. The three parts of this book have italicized "scenes" that are real life actual events of my life followed by an elaboration of that moment or time. I felt it was better to depict it as a story rather than merely telling you what was going on in my life. The scenes start from the earlier part of year 2016 and go backward chronologically to my high school experiences. I implore you to immerse yourself in the imagination of the events. Perhaps you can relate or know someone who may relate to the select scenes of my life. While many have endured several hardships, trials, and tribulations in life, my hope is that my story resonates with you in a way that lets you know your own story has victories in it too once you change your perspective.

You see, perspective has much to do with your response to life's circumstances. It all starts in the mind. If your thinking is whack, then the whole process may be daunting, devastating, or hard to recover from. My goal with sharing *parts* of my story in this book is to provide a base of the woman I am and to encourage someone that there is a light you can reach—that light is Jesus. The ugly part is walking it out. Sometimes the process is long while other times, it's short. Regardless, the process is still real. You find out more about yourself as an individual, others, and how life sets us up for meeting purpose and destiny.

My faith in God has been what has kept me through this process. All that I owe to my life can be found through the redemptive Blood of Jesus Christ. Without my Lord and

Savior Jesus Christ, I'd probably be in a mental institution somewhere, promiscuous because of low self-worth, or living life vicariously through the lens of lust and pride because of the battle wounds of hurt and pain. I thank the Father for saving me, marking me, choosing me, and calling me to partake in the works as an ambassador for the Kingdom of Heaven. While many are religious in nature as it pertains to such belief, I thank God for relationship.

PART ONE

"Now What?"

"Hey, girl, how are you?" she asked a friend who was in the real estate industry.

"I'm good, girl, how are you?" her friend asked. They had known each other since college and divinely their paths seemed to cross again.

"Is your office hiring for any staff vacancies?" she asked her friend hesitantly.

Their conversation ended with her telling her friend what just recently happened in hopes of understanding she had to act fast to secure a job position elsewhere. She had bills and as we all know, bills wait on no man—they just keep coming...so disrespectful, right? She called her trusted family member who took time to agree in prayer that God would order her next steps and moves. She then realized she had enough savings to secure all her personal financial obligations of which the biggest at the time was her mortgage. Her savings would last her a few months comfortably.

Prior to that conversation, she had received two prophecies two days in a row. Each prophecy lasted about 45 minutes to an hour and was congruent with one another. She didn't share with anyone what the prophecies were, but man were they BIG. Both had to do with real estate, business, platforms, advertising, marketing, family restoration, love life, etc. She remembered wondering why she would receive such great words of encouragement and edification at a time like this. Then suddenly, it hit her: She remembered that she had received a word of prophecy earlier that year. She scurried through her notebook to find it—she writes down all her prophetic words. And sure enough, it aligned with what the other two individuals spoke over her.

But it didn't stop there. The day after receiving her most recent prophetic word, she received a phone call. Surely, she was not expecting to receive yet another 45-minute word or more prophesy spoken over her life. She got off the phone on that third day (Friday) and just began to weep, crying out before the Lord for such promises spoken to encourage her during "the process." It was exactly 21 days from that day that she started her consecration before the Lord. March 2016 would end up being one of the most memorable times of her life. Little did she know, this process she was enduring was the start of some of the greatest transitions to come.

I know people have gone through worse things but being laid off was a big deal for me at this time in my life. I took time to seek the Lord and get in His presence. I remember my cousin saying, "It must be something major God needs to do with you because for Him to take you off your job, seemingly for no reason...wow." Sometimes we just need to change the way we think about the different *whys* of our life's circumstances. That was huge when I looked at it from a new perspective. **Perspective is a major game changer when it comes to facing challenges and hardships in life.**

Sometimes, God pushes us out of circumstances. Are you analytical and logical most times with your decisions? Unsure? Well, to be analytical means you typically like to use common sense or conceptualize a thing and consider all outcomes before making that decision. Whereas, logical thinkers typically like to state and simply deal with facts as to an anticipated outcome. We know that it takes the foolish things to confound the wise according to 1 Corinthians 1:27, right? God chooses to allow things to happen in our world to let us know we are not exempt from thinking we know it all or fully comprehended a thing; and it's not always the strongest who wins—it's those who endure until the end of a thing.

Even in considering my perspective about being laid off, it is not to be boastful more so than grateful God's grace and mercy was still with me *when*. I know you have a *when* in your life. You remember *when* you could've gotten pregnant, could've lost the house, could've been homeless, could've got that life sentence, could've lost your scholarship, could've contracted HIV or other STDs, could've not been chosen for the promotion, could've been left for dead, could've drowned in the water, could've died in the auto accident, could've married the wrong one, could've lost your mind…Oh, but there was a "but God" moment you can be thankful for!! Even if these events happened in your life, you overcame them. Yeah, you got a *when* if you think back over your life.

So, I can say, "Oh the termination—you know the demotion for a promotion—was a setup for where God needs me to be," but there is always room for development and growth too. Even during unwarranted circumstances, always seek to determine or evaluate your own actions and your own recourse of what you could have done differently to always remain in a place of humility for optimal growth in life. In other words, some things are necessary to go through simply because God can trust you to stay the course so His glory may be revealed in your life. There are also, however, times when you must determine *could I have* been more adamant about my roles and responsibilities? According to 1 Corinthians 10:31, "whatsoever ye do, do all to the glory of God," and this includes how we perform on the job as an example of seeking to serve in an excellent manner in all things we do.

Now, (the) Holy Spirit told me, "Wait for Me to start looking for a job." So over the next 21 days, my spiritual life changed tremendously. I found myself deeper in worship, deeper in reading my Word, and hearing God's voice much clearer while being exposed to His undying and unconditional love for me. It was the most gratifying experience that superseded the issues of not having a job (plus I had my emergency fund on lock). I remember talking with God the same way I would sit and have casual conversations with a friend. We'd laugh, He'd have jokes (yeah, He told me to go to Hezekiah 4 one night—I looked crazy looking for it too), I'd cry, He'd comfort me, I'd praise and worship Him, and His presence would fill my home. There was so much peace in my house. My home was my safe haven. I created a natural atmosphere where (the) Holy Spirit would dwell there *with* me and not only *in* me. I could feel the presence of angels in my home.

What God was showing me was to count it all joy when I walk into diverse temptations (James 1:2). Society has made persons, places, and things take the place of the presence of God in our lives so much so that in the season when we are unfrequented, remote, or seemingly isolated, we don't even acknowledge God's presence. I wonder how hurtful that is to Him. It is imperative that individuals learn to seek Him daily and read the Word of God that it may expose the tactics of the enemy so when we *feel* alone, we know that God's Word is true in that He will never leave us nor forsake us (Hebrews 13:5). Let me make note that this was not the first time I ever felt like I was alone. I will share later where loneliness had me feeling depressed and suicidal (so keep reading), but the difference between being alone and loneliness was important to mention. Sometimes we think we have mastered something within our character or personality only to be tried later and realize, "Oh, wow, I'm dealing with this again." Once I acknowledged Jesus and gathered understanding of this process, I found myself to be happier than I had ever been in quite some time, especially since being laid off.

Now, I consider myself to be a social butterfly and I can get along with anyone but this newfound love for being "alone" was the joy I received from going through *the process*. I found myself in love with Jesus more than I had ever been. I could leave out for the day and come home and feel the presence of God waiting for me when I walked through the door. There are no words to express this relationship…I just knew it was without a shadow of doubt real. Together, the Lord and I were growing by leaps and bounds. When you develop a true relationship with God, your flesh *can* fall subject to the will of your spirit every time; and temptations, trials, and unwarranted circumstances become that much easier to overcome.

Sometimes in the process of a transition, others may not understand and in some regard, serve as a hindrance or distraction to the process. I had just previously left the church ministry I was a member of at the time and could only imagine someone thinking that as a result of me *leaving,* now an unfortunate circumstance happens. That was the enemy at work on the battlefield of my mind trying to stagnate and cause me to question the process God had me to embark upon. Knowing whether circumstances are a God-intended thing can sometimes be hard when what is going on is new to you. Having the gift of discernment can help mitigate any negative seeds by use of wisdom and words in love. When we carnally look at what is happening in our lives (or the lives of others), we tend to miss the *bigger picture* being so focused on the *right now* or the *right way* all because it doesn't look like what we thought it should. Walking by faith and not by sight (2 Corinthians 5:7) is so important when being processed for His glory.

You may come to a crossroad where you must ask yourself, now what? It's during these times of seemingly being overwhelmed by the unknown that your perspective must change in order to get from where you are to where God may be trying to take you.

"Wow! That Was Quick!"

March 11, 2016, was the day that thrusted her towards her next place of destiny. She walked into work like any other day. A friend stopped by the leasing office seemingly to want nothing.

What was surprising was that her friend told her, "You know you are not going to be here much longer, right?"

She without hesitation asserted, "Yeah, girl, the first opportunity that presents itself, I'm putting in my two-week notice," as she threw up the deuce sign and laughed jokingly.

Well, to her surprise that "not much longer" moment happened that day. Closer to the end of the work day, the newest property manager called her in the back of the office. While looking sad, the manager said, "I'm sorry but corporate is letting you go."

Without hesitation, she said "Ok." The manager gave her no reason as to why and quite surprisingly at the time, she didn't ask. Gathering her belongings and things from around her desk, what just took place didn't bother her. She gave the maintenance supervisor some keys for a tenant who was moving into a unit. She left a file on the desk of the leasing agent and explained to the manager which stack of checks had yet to be deposited into the batch order for tenant accounts. Yes, you guessed it: she was still working. She said goodbye to the remaining staff and proceeded to her car as she realized the relief that came with the incident. But then it hit her, "Why was I just let go?" She immediately called her now former supervisor on her cell phone and inquired about the same thing some of you would've probably asked up front.

The supervisor replied with, "They gave no reason as to why they are letting you go, and I wish I would've had more time to work with you."

Hearing that made her feel more relieved. Perhaps it wasn't performance so much rather than them wanting to revamp their demographics or create a "new persona" of the office staff. That was ok with her. She was the longest standing employee there, giving of her time and self while feeling her season had come to an end.

Have you ever been pushed into or out of something? Before being let go, I knew for several months my season there was up. But God knew that out of fear and slothfulness—trying to analyze things (which I do often)—that I was not going to move in the time He needed me to. So, He pushed me out. **Sometimes God will do us like that...push us out of what was comfortable to get us to meet our destiny**. I used to say to the Lord in prayer, "God, I either have to make more money working the same hours or make the same amount of money working less hours, but something has got to give." I repeated this often and my routine became monotonous. I knew I wanted to do more for God's kingdom. I wanted more time to work on personal business desires such as real estate or my consulting/leadership business, writing books, helping others, and simply being more accessible for Him.

By the time I would get home from work, I was too tired most days to complete assignments for my MBA program on top of leadership roles in ministry—and let's not forget my "three amigos" aka my children. To say the least, I was stretching myself thin and the struggle became real. However, I was content because this job was meeting my immediate needs. I knew what I was getting every two weeks on my paycheck, I knew what my schedule was going to be, etc. **I was content, or satisfied, although I felt constrained.**

Many of you reading this right now may acknowledge that you have felt or currently feel the same way if you do some self-reflection. Often, you may find yourself staying in careers, jobs, relationships, ministries, geographical locations or places of residence longer than God's intent for you. This usually happens because it's harder to do something you've never done out of fear that it might not work. **The time it takes you to get through your process is simply how much time you take to think differently.** Part of being a good steward requires knowing how to manage ourselves with the time we are given by knowing what season we are in and being obedient in it.

Businesses, for example, may not do well in the growth phase of the business life-cycle because the right development and plan was not implemented during the introduction phase. Frustration that is derived from being constrained can be from trying to execute when you should be planning and vice versa. Surely, that would frustrate anyone. I knew my season was up or that it was coming to an end, but I was just too comfortable to prepare myself for the transition for fear of the unknown. So, what did God do? He pushed me out and gave me no other choice, time, or option but to get ready. **My purpose was stagnated while I was staying comfortable**. That season and job had served its purpose in my life, but I was still holding on to the familiar. How could I ever grow and blossom if I was not willing to change my surroundings or my thinking and perception? I even had a lady tell me, "You are so much greater than this job," as if she even knew I was out of place.

And *you* know you should've left that job/career a long time ago. You knew it was time to move and get out from under your "safety net" and get out of your "comfort zone." You knew the relationship was not good for you when you realized you both wanted very different paths in life or that instead of you helping that person elevate, they delayed or stagnated your growth in the vision God had given you. But you stayed anyway and sometimes, for the wrong reason. **You are your most important person. If you don't take care of yourself, you cannot expect to effectively tend to the needs of another.**

We are told to have faith in all things, right? To abound and be abased, right? In your going out and in your coming in, right? You must visualize what you are hoping for or have faith in. Next, you must write down what you see; create some visual you can see regularly that keeps you encouraged. Then, the next most important step is to execute your faith with works; you must actively engage and do something. *James 2:26 For as the body without the spirit is dead, so faith without works is dead also.* You see, faith is movement. Faith doesn't work unless it's in a constant form of movement. It's conceived in the mind, expressed through the words you speak, and then it moves through the "members" of your body so that faith is manifested in your life. You see how that works? It won't become fully manifested until you do something.

Various experiences in your life will be the prerequisite for gaining a new level of faith—*yes, there are levels to this thing called faith.* So, I knew I had to do something when I got laid off from my full-time job, but *what* was the question. At the time, I had a bachelor's degree and was working on my master's degree; so of course, getting another job was going to be easy, right? My layoff was a setup for me to focus on personal development as it pertains to discipline, consistency, and diligence. I must say that I am still learning and honing these skillsets and am truly thankful for the growth in those areas, but I have much growing yet to do. Remember, it's a *process.*

"You Told Me Ahead of Time"

It was Wednesday morning, March 9, 2016, and she woke up to write down a summary of the dream she had the night before—at least what she remembered—and it read:

> *"dream 3.8.16 had a dream where there was a new management company that bought us or/and we were all going to be replaced. Really different dream. The complex was huge."*

She snuggled back under the covers and laid quietly in her bed to rationalize the dream to gather its significance. Before she knew it, she found herself asleep again after assuring herself with, "I won't fall into a deep sleep; I'll be sure to get back up in five minutes."

Suddenly, as she violently swings the covers back, she screams, "Oh, no!" She hurried herself to dash out of the house for work, leaving the thoughts of the dream behind.

Don't act like this has never happened to you. You know you have hit the snooze button a couple of times and declared you were just going to "rest your eyes" a bit before getting out of bed only to look and see how bright the light was coming into your room, signifying you know you were late for work or school. Not to mention, you utterly forgot about the dream you had just written down. I had that dream in 2016 but let me take you back a bit to help you understand why.

I worked at a distressed 242-unit apartment community as an assistant property manager. I got hired as a leasing specialist in December 2013. Among other professions prior to this, I had worked as a pharmacy technician, family care counselor, rehabilitation therapist, and administrative assistant. It was safe to say I had the customer skills necessary to perform well on the job but for the first three weeks, I felt a bit overwhelmed with the new role. Perhaps because other than the manager, I was the only leasing staff there for several weeks learning the new tasks and performing to corporate's expectations. However, as time went on, I picked up things quickly and felt quite comfortable. I honed skills necessary for working in the apartment industry such as dealing with irate tenants, touring the property with new prospects, communicating effectively with vendors, and providing the best customer service to the residents of the community as possible. Six months into the position, I found myself being promoted to the assistant property manager and I was excited to learn new things concerning the apartment industry. I had moved from the open leasing area to a small office up front.

Although I liked my job, management seemed to change every quarter (*slight* exaggeration but basically). The turnover rate was alarming; I witnessed at least 15 different employees come and go since working there. I remember feeling like my purpose there was to help influence others in the best positive, godly way possible. Some residents confided in me some of their deepest inner secrecies and trusted me with that information, whether it was sexuality, death of a loved one, relationship/marital issues, family, or even self-image. I felt blessed to be considered someone many could trust. There are a few to this very day whom I have built lasting connections with and keep in touch from time to time.

"To Die or Not to Die"

She wrote a letter dated February 12, 2016; the Lord told her it had to be written by the end of the week to be given by that Sunday. She knew what it felt like to suffer the repercussions of being moved by her emotions, so she acted faster than usual as to be under the obedience of the Lord. An excerpt read:

> *"While we all get connected with people, share thoughts, visions, and ideas, fellowship, and interact, we should never let that comfortability keep us from moving towards our destinies in the Body of Christ. On that notion, I must move on to the next chapter of my life's journey that God has for me to complete. This notice in no wise disconnects me from the members...as we are all part of the same body."*

She remembered how she paced back and forth trying to reason within herself about the unction to leave the ministry. She knew God was telling her it's time to leave, but what would others think? The members had become family to her, people she considered to be close with. It was hard because naturally, she knew the importance of being dedicated, loyal, and committed. She knew what it meant to be dependable and trustworthy. It was a hard thing to do but she also knew if she stayed any longer, the toxicity would have destroyed her. As much as she loved the people she had grown such a connection with, her spirit had been utterly vexed. The first letter was dated January 10, 2016 (approximately a month earlier), and an excerpt read:

> *"It is my regard to inform you of my decision to relinquish my responsibility as an active auxiliary leader with the Praise and Worship ministry. My desire is to see the efforts that have been established or set in place may continue with the co-leader and remaining members to effectively continue with the gifts God has placed in all of them. My sincere hope is that you understand my proposition and collaboratively, we can still move forward with ministry efforts. Please except my continued prayers and encouragement with the efforts of the ministry to minister to the total man and win souls for Christ."*

She knew the day would come when she would need to "let go," but didn't realize it would come from an

33

unwarranted place. It was hard trying to lead others knowing the craftiness that was going on behind the scenes. She could no longer allow herself to declare the glory of the Lord in that atmosphere; she was more concerned about how God received her than man. She had to pull away lest she died from the imprisonment of bondage her mind was entrapped in.

She remembered when she lifted her head, after her face was buried in her hands, to gaze out and see the cemented monument that was across the street from the plaza in which she had parked her car that day. Her vision was blurred from the water that swelled in her eyes as a tear rolled down her left cheek first and then her right. She remembered it just as (the) Holy Spirit revealed to her how she was going to be tried inappropriately, asking, "But why me, Lord?" She pondered why she had to go through and experience the grief and pain that came from an evil spirit seeking to impregnate her heart with furious anger and seeds that would naturally battle against forgiveness. On three separate occasions, the Lord showed her how the enemy would try her and what exactly would be said or done; and sure enough, it happened EXACTLY that way. Inasmuch as doing what she had always seemingly knew to do which was to "be resilient," she proceeded to smile and considered showing love even if it meant she suffered in "the process."

Many people leave ministries for various reasons such as relocation to another city, poor leadership, toxicity or lack of spiritual growth, the infamous "church hurt," or lack of commitment, loyalty and honor. Perhaps the ministry no longer had the capacity to carry the weight of glory that would be revealed in a person's life. What about obedience, though (of which is the most important), even when you don't want to go? Maybe the person has completed their assignment to that ministry, and it is time to move on. Every experience, good or bad, has personally helped me have a better understanding about self-awareness, people, and the spiritual realm as it pertains to this Christian journey—my faith walk. I am a firm believer that love covers a multitude of sin (1 Peter 4:8); and I also believe in righteous rebuke where exposure is necessary (Matthew 16:23).

Right before I was laid off my job, I resigned from my former ministry with the letters from the scene above. There was so much going on from a spiritual perspective and I knew within myself that something had to give. Many people *in general* have been in a place of transition as it pertains to ministry over the last several years. The current prophetic alignment of the paradigm shift that is currently going on in today's world requires the church to get ready first for the world to enter and receive global revival. In reference to the dispensation of time, transition is quite necessary for that shift to happen. Transition gives you the ability to stretch what may be unknown to the capacity within you to accomplish a certain thing in your life. Can you think of a time you were feeling the nudging of (the) Holy Spirit to leave or transition out of a ministry into where God was leading you? Now, I'm not talking about leaving a ministry based on emotions or because of a reproach you received. You need to learn emotional/spiritual maturity as it pertains to that. Your character is built when if you want to leave—with rightful regard to do so—you don't.

Doing what doesn't always feel good is one way to know you are growing; but I'm talking about being led of the Lord to leave—there is a huge difference. If I may suggest a nugget: never leave a thing regardless of what it is until your assignment in that place has been completed. An uncompleted assignment is just as bad as delayed obedience, which is disobedience altogether. The problem is that many people cannot recognize when a season has ended (or began), which has much to do with life's frustrations. Here are a few ways one can determine if the ministry they're in is toxic to the point where (the) Holy Spirit, God Himself, is leading you to transition:

Reasons to Leave a Ministry	Reasons Not to Leave a Ministry
If there is physical, spiritual, verbal, sexual, and/or emotional abuse not appropriately dealt with	You've been reproved about a thing and it initially offends you
You seek help from leadership but never receive it	Your focus is more on the wrong of others rather than the posture of your own heart
Your church is a cult	You don't want to do what the leader has established because you feel there is a better way
Leadership is toxic to your spiritual growth	You are growing spiritually in your personal walk with the Lord and in your faith
You have no opportunity to serve and grow in your gifts	You are serving in areas that focus on your gifts to the church as a whole
When your spiritual appetite is no longer being fed and your assignment has been fulfilled	There's a godly provoke from others to reevaluate the posture of your heart
When the church worries more about politics rather than Jesus	Your assignment to edify and build up that ministry is not finished (regardless of how you feel) especially if sent there by God

Funds to the ministry in which you sow are misappropriated	The leader, ministry, and members are prospering (this is ok; prosperity is a good thing)
A leader makes sexual gestures/advances/conversations towards you that are inappropriate	
Gifts of prophecy are used as a cover for manipulation, control, etc.	
Something doesn't sit right in your spirit and you know or can sense something is wrong	

My ex-husband and I had been separated and divorced by the time I were led to leave the ministry we attended and knew I had grown in so many more ways than one. I've never been a fan of "ministry-hopping;" it is just as bad as an individual "job-hopping." You can't focus on skills and abilities and gain experience that builds personal development and character when you are so easily swayed by the next ministry looking for it to be more "perfect."

Have you heard of the story of the pastor and the complaining woman? Well, the story is about a lady who tells her pastor she was leaving the church because of the hypocrites, gossiping, wrong lifestyles, and phone usage in service of the church she attends. So the pastor asks her to take a full cup of water and walk around the church three times before leaving. Thinking nothing to it, the lady does it and comes back to the pastor still ready to leave. The last thing he asked of her was if she had seen any of the things that she told him about as to why she was leaving. Her response was "no." His explanation to her was because she was so focused on making sure the water in her cup didn't spill, she didn't have time to look to see what everyone else was doing. There's a great moral to this story. I share it because people have got to be committed to working out their own soul salvation (Philippians 2:12).

There are two types of churchgoers today: Those who go to church to be edified and those who are there to help edify—and what a double prize if you are experiencing both at the same ministry. Knowing which "season" you are in is vital to determining whether you should leave a ministry or not. Frankly, before you join a ministry, you should be led by (the) Holy Spirit to plant your feet. God may tell you to join in fellowship with a ministry because of an assignment He has graced you to be able to do there; in that case, do it. There will be trials, circumstances, and tribulations in life you will experience and being part of the right ministry is vital to overcoming those experiences (even if the "going through" is *because* of a ministry). Nothing is more disheartening than members of a ministry going through life-changing circumstances and the church can't help and may add to the dismay.

Many may relate this to the infamous phrase, "church hurt." There are several people today who don't attend a physical church because of a negative experience that even left them questioning their faith by those in a church. But the *church* didn't hurt you, an individual or group of individuals did. We must remember that pastors, ministers, and leaders of the church are people too, and they are not exempt from the temptations of the enemy. You shouldn't blame that one bad experience on the Body of Christ as a whole…I didn't.

You see, it takes a grace from on high to be able to receive from someone operating out of their anointing or gifting—because gifts come without repentance (Romans 11:29)—all while knowing of a sin they may have committed against you or others. I was exasperated too many times within my spirit from an individual who was supposed to be righteously leading and stewarding the flock. It's important not to engage in gossip and the slandering of people's name or character. Truth be told, as I have seen stated on social media, most people's reputation is saved because someone else decided not to share their side of the story.

No one church is perfect; however, there ought to be a standard. That standard ALWAYS starts with the head first just as with a husband in a marriage leading his family. First Corinthians 14:40 tells us to "let all things be done decently and in order": Not "some" things; not "certain" things; not "important" things; not "favorable" things; but ALL things. There is a standard that comes with ministering effectively; a standard when counseling; a standard with sharing information, including feelings; and a standard in relationships, especially in the church. There is a key word in this scripture that I must point out: *Let*…such a powerful three-letter word. "Let" in this text simply means *to allow, to stretch or spread out, to permit.* Everything you do—be it serving as a leader in a church, an employer or employee, a parent, a teacher within a school system, a husband or wife, or any role within your life—do with decency and integrity.

As a result of this experience, I have grown passionate about the trusted outlets leaders need too. They need to be encouraged to not give up or throw in the towel when things get heavy in the process of leading others while attending to personal needs. Many ministries do not prosper simply because some of the most rudimentary measures and principles of establishing order is not adhered to in leaders' personal lives/homes and thus, reflects in their leadership. In contrast, leaders will sometimes place more significance and importance on their role in the church instead of confronting those issues in the home. That's not good either. **God looks**

at marriage, family, and ministry with the same regard and importance—starting with marriage being your first "ministry."

Congregants or members must also remember that your leaders are individuals with a grave responsibility on their shoulders of how well they steward the development of your spiritual growth. They are human and experience the same emotions as would anyone else. They will be tried with the desires of their own lust or heart, the pride of life, and temptations they have not experienced true deliverance from. Praying *for* your leaders is as important as you requesting prayer from them.

Balance is so important. It is vital that we are not so heavenly-minded that we are no earthly good and vice versa. Being balanced will require team leaders to be in place to tend to the functions and operations of the ministry while the lead pastor/overseer is away. **Trust must be established and the need to be in control relinquished.** Every great leader knows that those who are part of the leadership team help cover areas of weaknesses when a big vision has been openly shared. Additionally, your own spiritual discipline as a believer and member of a ministry is important to ensure you are not idolizing man over God. Your level of intimacy with the Lord will cause you to live a life of purity before Him, in front of others, and behind closed doors. Too many people representing the Body of Christ are operating in their gifts, yet the grace of God has lifted. But because the Father loves His children so much, He'll discipline even the most influential individuals to help them get it together before eternal damnation is their fate.

A healthy soul is important. Inner healing and self-forgiveness must take place in order to lead effectively. If you don't know what inner healing and self-forgiveness looks like, please go ask your leaders. If they can't provide instruction, then perhaps they themselves need it as much as you. They should be able to help in this area, even if that means pointing you in the right direction to the person who can help. What's the use of serving in ministry for the

Kingdom's sake, cultivating a relationship with the Lord, or having an expectation of others and it's not clearly expressed or seen in your own everyday life how you are overcoming battles and temptations of the enemy? I'm not talking about having to endure in longsuffering the issues of life sometimes, but rather practicing what you teach or preach.

Being in the will of God is important. **Ministries should be launching with God's stamp of approval**...not because of what someone said you should be doing, what you feel like doing, or because it seems to be the "in" thing to monetize and capitalize on as a business. People belong to God, not a leader. I've been resilient for a reason in my life—not by my own strength, might, or wit but through the power and strength of (the) Holy Spirit. People who are typically called to a high place in the spirit realm are seemingly tested the most through tough trials and tribulations. It doesn't make them greater than the next person. They may just have to be processed a bit longer for the call required of them. I am eternally grateful to partake in the sufferings with Christ, even from the Church.

"And Scene"

It doesn't matter where you are in your life, there are always "processes" taking place that get you from one place to the next as it pertains to purpose and destiny. There are sets of predestined experiences that will happen, and then there are experiences that happen out of our own will for either something we do/did or the lack thereof. Either way, you will go through the process. Sometimes it's not necessarily the process itself that may seem hard but your perspective while enduring it. Have you ever been in a line (let's say at lunch as a teenager in high school) and you got pushed while waiting to grab your plate (whether intentionally or not), and it made you feel some type of way? You may have felt embarrassed, frustrated, or responded well/poorly in the moment. Well, that's what being "processed" sometimes may feel like. It is during these times of testing in life that you are being pushed into the next level of your personal greatness. Ok, so I'm sure you can think of some other examples, but you get what I am saying. What is needed for your development from going through the process is essential for that personal growth—greatness. Just remember, it all starts with a mindset.

PART TWO

"The Faith Walk"

"I need to take an extended lunch today," she would express to her supervisor or the property manager of the apartment complex.

"I'm headed there now," she would say as she drove out of the complex talking to her realtor.

She started taking extended lunches without saying too much as to why. She went looking at different homes in the community with her realtor. One day upon returning to the office, it dawned on her that she was putting works with the faith; she had always been declaring IT WON'T BE LIKE THIS ALWAYS. It made her heart smile; and to think, she was motivated to do so by the people who motivated her the most: her children.

She was coming up on two years since moving back in with her mom. She didn't want to (who wants to ever need to move back home) but if it meant being able to see her kids more often, it was well worth the sacrifice. Not to mention, she was practically homeless and needed to get back on her feet since divorcing her husband. One day, going into the back room of that old single-wide trailer—a room a little bigger than most standard-sized bathrooms—she realized, this can't be it. To this very day, she still has the picture embedded in her mind (and literally) of all three of her children sleeping in one twin bed. It was that night she silently worshipped, cried, and prayed to the Lord to change her circumstances by giving her a strategy and the next thing to do.

Now, consider the above scene and ask yourself if you have ever said any or all of the below phrases during the course of your life and perhaps, still today:

"I can't wait until I become a homeowner"	"This is my year"
"I'm going higher"	"My greater is before me"
"Something has got to give"	"I've got to do more, have more"
"Prosperity and favor are upon me"	"This is my season"
"This time, I'm going to do it"	"I don't care who's with me"
I'll go Lord; send me"	"I can do this"

The interesting thing about these seemingly motivational phrases is that they require a response by movement. It's ok to be content; however, knowing when to *move* is as vital. I remember taking a few months to save money to purchase a vehicle. I wanted an all-black, three-row, all-leather, midsize SUV. I simply told the Lord my desire, had a dream confirming what I wanted and within a couple of months, was able to purchase that vehicle in cash. There was something about an all-black vehicle that I thought was sexy. I didn't even have much negotiating to do because the seller took $1K off the original price without me even asking: FAVOR. I have never in all my few decades of life had an auto loan for a car. I have, however, saved money, driven to South Florida and bought vehicles cash.

We know to declare stuff like "this is my season" and "I'm going higher" or "greater is before me." While these personal "uplifting" declarations are great, there is more to merely speaking them. I was separated/divorced from my husband and seemingly gained more as a redefined, focused single woman than I did while married even though we know that two is better than one. My motivation (my children) led me to have a vision, which led to the movement needed to see that vision come into fruition. We know how to speak those things that are not as if they were as it is written according to Romans 4:17. We also know we cannot please God without faith (Hebrews 11:6) and that faith with no works is dead (James 2:26).

Not necessarily planned, I gave myself a birthday present for me and my children…a home. My birthday in

2015 was one of the greatest moments of my life. I moved in silence and boom, I was a homeowner before I knew it. Now, I've always been a saver of my money, considered myself to be a good financial steward (with room for growth and improvement), and I was always willing to learn to increase my wealth capacity. My goal in my home purchase was to start the plans of leaving a legacy for my children and the generations thereafter.

The first thing I had to do was determine what I would get qualified for, and I started by talking to a representative of member services at my credit union. This initial step for many people won't even be accomplished. **We are so consumed with "waiting" on the promise that we forget to do "our part" so that God can do His**. Another reason behind this is fear—fear of the unknown, especially for single-income household earners. Fear will derail your greatest of blessings.

Then came the thoughts the enemy formed that tried to keep me from moving forward such as "you know your credit is not A1" or "you can't take your children with you; you're going to miss them greatly" or "you don't even have your own family supporting your transition." John 10:10 states that Ole Lucy (Satan, Lucifer, our adversary) comes to steal, kill, and destroy; but we know Jesus came that we may have life and have it more abundantly. Real estate investing is one of the greatest forms of wealth creation you can partake in for yourself and your family. Whether it is flipping homes, wholesaling, becoming a realtor and helping buyers/sellers, or simply investing to hold properties to receive residual income and become a landlord. Investing in real estate is paramount and should be on your list of multiple streams of income. Wealth-building, leaving a legacy, and financial protocols is a whole other topic that I've personally grown to indulge in and be adamant about.

I was so proud of myself! My bills were always paid on time and I was saving my money—I hope saving is part of your financial plan too. It took me about two months to get this major debt off my credit in order to move forward for getting a better loan amount and rate on my mortgage. I wouldn't have known that if I was too fearful, thinking I may not qualify or trying to wait until all my ducks were in a row. I knew that if I didn't want to see my children sleeping in the same twin bed together for the lack of space in my mother's home, then I needed to bust a move, literally.

What I thought I had lost from the divorce, God gave me that plus more and even in a short period of time. Remember, faith without works is dead. So let me offer a word of encouragement for those who are too scared to jump out into the deep or do something that you've never done before: If you are ever going to get to where you desire to go, you must first assess to see how far away you are from reaching that goal. I'm not going to tell you to write down all your SMART goals (goals that are specific, measurable, attainable, realistic/relevant, and time-based) nor am I going to tell you to speak this hefty list of affirmations daily over your life (although you can/should do both). But what I am going to say is that if you want to see the enemy flee from your life, you must resist him (James 4:7). To resist doesn't mean you turn your head as if you don't acknowledge that he is coming against you. Resistance must serve as a defensive maneuver or actionable gesture against the enemy; it literally looks like striving against or opposing in some manner that what is against you.

Let's digress to paint a visual of what resisting the enemy looks like. I had a dream one day that I was outside at nighttime (significant of warfare for me). I remember these black dogs (demonic) barking at me. Well, one of those dogs was viciously gnarling and barking at me with saliva and foam coming out of its mouth while showing all its teeth to try to illicit fear in me or cause me to run so it could attack (with its two other homies in the background). So the dog is up on its hind legs with his front two legs wrapped around my two arms as if we were in a brawl arm lock (you guys know what I'm trying to explain). So now he's in my face and as he is still barking and growling at me, my teeth are seemingly closed tight but I'm saying to him, "Get off of me," but I'm not scared, moved, or fearful. I'm literally saying, "Get off me now," with a mean expression on my face (like "you don't run nothing over here"). Have you ever seen two people about to fight and one person flinches at the other and it makes the other person jump? Well, that's what I did with this dog even though we were in much closer proximity. It felt like this dog was in my face for an extremely long period of time. Finally, the dog got down after he saw that I wasn't scared because I was *resisting* him.

Now, I knew the dream was demonic in nature and I knew the interpretation upon waking; so I immediately went into prayer over my destiny and future, thanking God for the victory. Listen, you must be intentional in your pursuits of fighting against the enemy. He will try in every dimension of wellness (spiritual, financial, intellectual, physical, social, emotional) of your life to attack, sabotage, delay, and destroy you any way that he can. He doesn't care about your big home, fancy cars, your popularity, or even what success you can obtain in this life; he is concerned about your soul—

that's his most prized possession. Your soul is more valuable than anything else in this world to him.

One of the biggest spiritual weapons of demonic influence the enemy uses is fear. Fear is crippling, stagnating, and draining if you entertain it. You've got to first believe that God has not given you the spirit of fear but of power, love, and a sound mind (2 Timothy 1:7); for we know there is no fear in love, but perfect love casts out fear (1 John 4:18).

In order to become victorious in your resistance to the enemy's attacks of intimidation or fear so that he may flee, you must **SUBMIT YOURSELF TO GOD**. That's the first call to action in James 4:7. Many people like to quote the second half but forget the first part of the verse. Submitting yourself to God simply requires obedience. Submission via obedience automatically distances the enemy. That's not to say that weapons won't be formed against you, but know that they won't prosper (Isaiah 54:17). I don't care if it is moving to an unfamiliar geographical location, leaving a ministry, starting a business that provides a service, developing a product, changing the type of friends you surround yourself

with, finding the strength to say no or courage to say yes,

buying a home, or simply changing the way you

think…never be afraid to walk the path that increases your

faith.

"The Driven Choice"

She knew that since receiving the release of "the decision," she was permitted to move forward. She drove 45 minutes to the location. That was enough time for her to think, reconsider, and make peace with the decision that was before her. She couldn't believe it but deep down, she knew she was making the right choice. She wanted this story to end differently. She drove in silence as her mind took her on a roller coaster ride of all that had happened leading up to this point. This was not supposed to happen—not to her—she thought as she drove down Interstate 75 heading south bound. She thought about how others would perceive how "faith filled" she was, always professing that things were going to turn around in their favor. What would people think about her now? Would she have to explain herself to others? Maybe an ounce of hope was all she knew she needed before going further with the decision that would later serve as the new beginning her life needed.

Wow! Me of all people…I'm about to be a divorced

woman. I decided to seek for the right divorce attorney after

that conversation, knowing I was released from that

individual. I remember a weight being lifted off me, which

was a usual sign that I was making the right decision after being in the valley of decision for approximately two years. I saw this billboard sign about divorce for $199 and I was like, "Oh, that's reasonable." My divorce shouldn't be too much to negotiate and mediate on because we didn't have any vehicles, property, businesses, or accounts in our name jointly.

My attorney informed me that she and her husband had been in the "divorce business" for years and they felt it was their ministry. Wait a minute! Ministry!?! Did I hear that right? She shared stories of people who would come into their office and they literally would be able to help save their marriage. I got excited, as I knew this must be divine that I connected with her. Perhaps she would also tell me whether I was making the right decision. Naturally, I'm a private person because I don't believe in tainting someone else's story and thus, don't want mine to be tainted either. So I told her my story in part; and I remember her looking at me like, "Oh my, you seem like such a nice young lady…to have experienced that at such a young age." She would share bits of her other clients' stories but didn't express to me that I shouldn't go through with it. She implied otherwise...that sometimes we try to hold on to something even when God wants us to let it go.

Once I made the decision to move forward with her services, **I knew the choice was going to be liberating even though I didn't want to go through the process**. God was about to take me through this process of solely depending on Him, even when others didn't understand how God was guiding me. I didn't always understand either; it was embarrassing to say the least, but I thank God for those individuals who were vital to my process at that time in my life. I didn't feel the need to explain myself to anyone and I thank God that He kept me through that process...and is yet keeping me.

"The Decision"

She had now realized that this was necessary. It wasn't a hard decision to make once she received the release and answer, although it went against her initial desire. As

*some time passed leading into the end of the two years
separated from her husband, she began to ask God, "Lord,
why am I feeling like this?" as if this feeling was not part of
"her" will. She started to lose love for someone most people
would've lost love for a long time ago due to the
circumstance he caused in her life. In fact, many believe or
said that she had chosen a man over her own children. And
while she understood the logic to such reasoning, she knew
what God showed her in dreams and the prophetic words she
received was worth the wait.*

    *What she didn't know was that she was being
processed for something even greater. God gives us time and
when we don't do what we are supposed to within that
graced time, we suffer the consequences. Her husband had
time and perhaps because of what had dominion over him
spiritually, he chose not to change and perhaps didn't know
how. From being favored to losing their children to now the
loss of their marriage, her life had taken very sharp turns.
God told him that if he didn't stop lying and mistreating his
wife, He would take it all away—and that was exactly what
He allowed to happen.*

"Lord, don't let me lose my love for him." Wow! I

remember saying that phrase far too often over the course of

those two years. While "out of sight, out of mind" is a true

idiom, absence was supposed to make the heart grow fonder.

My husband at the time had done a year in the local county

jail for being found guilty as the alleged perpetrator of child

abuse and medical neglect…a family case. We had been

separated for two years and even after all that had happened,

I stayed. It sounds like the craziest thing, almost stupid if you ask the majority. But the more time has lapsed, I've grown to understand the necessity behind IT ALL. I had more compassion for this man for what it must feel like for him than I cared for my own emotional well-being. Plus, I wanted to be that biblical, ethical wife and honor my marital vows "for better or worse, in sickness and in health, for richer or for poorer…" because I wanted the Lord to know that I took them seriously and that I understood that two become one once you enter covenant.

Can one person save a marriage? Is that even possible? Why, absolutely. How, you wonder? With some patience from within, guidance from the Lord, unwavering love, a consistently strong prayer life and *freewill or choice,* a marriage indeed can be saved through the actions of one. Is it a hard task? Absolutely, but it's possible. Sometimes the pain of staying and waiting is seemingly worse than letting it all go. While the task can be hard and the emotional roller coaster ride frequent, I am convinced that God will get the glory out of your story the way He wants to if you are willing and obedient.

Now this is not my story, but I don't condone divorce just because divorce *is* part of my story. I remember growing up that my dad used to say, "If it gets too hot in the kitchen, you got to get out." I don't know if you've ever heard this phrase before but it means that if you are involved in something (or relationship) and the heat/pressure causes unwarranted actions or it's getting too much to deal with to where you are acting out of character or endangering your own life (or the lives of others), then get out at least until the fire cools.

One warm day when I was riding home, which was about a 30-minute commute at the time because I was living with my mother, I recall having a conversation that I deemed as *the* conversation with the Lord concerning my marriage. I was just talking, expressing my feelings and my emotions, communing with the Lord and thinking that I never would've thought I would have experienced what I was going through in a million years. I candidly remember telling the Lord that I was willing to wait for the restoration of my marriage (and eventually family) even if it took the next five to seven years. I was willing to wait if it meant He would get the glory out of my life—my story. I always knew that nothing was too hard for the Lord…nothing. The immediate response that I received from the Lord was, "But I'm not that kind of God." Whoa! As a rush of water filled my eyes, tears fell as I experienced this overwhelming overflow of the Father's liquid love overtake my being and every moral fiber in my body as I was caught up in a wind of emotional peace. It was the most satisfying feeling ever—it was my release—and that peace made my release freeing. I was liberated in that moment.

There are testimonies in the earth where God literally shows proof of Himself doing the miraculous in the lives of those who've had to endure major hard circumstances and hardships in life. I wanted all the biblical truths for waiting, staying, and honestly, I simply wanted to be in the will of the

Lord as it pertained to the Word of God and marriage. I searched for the answers through others even after getting in the Word. I wanted to understand. So not only did I seek out the answer, but I waited. I waited! Yeah, something most of us don't like to do. I'm that "ride or die" kind of person.

Remember I had to get fired (pushed) from my job. I had to see my kids sleeping in a twin bed, which ignited fire in my feet to purchase my first initial property (pushed). And now, I had feelings that I prayed against (pushed) into another emotional space so I could ultimately experience "the new" in my life. Now Matthew 19:6 tells us that what God has put or joined together, let no man put asunder or separate or pull apart. Perhaps someone told you that you cannot marry again unless you are reconciled back to your former spouse or not until that person dies. Let's delve into this matter, shall we, because for far too long have many (predominately the church folk) made individuals believe the Word in partial truths. We must stop taking the scripture out of context and using it as a manipulative tool for bondage and to validate excuses. There are other reasons than adultery for people to rightfully get divorced.

Let's first make very clear that one's personal conviction compared to that of another may be different. I'm not bound to the law; I therefore act accordingly. However, the fulfillment of the law (through the redemptive Blood of Jesus) does not dismiss the principle of the law in which it was created. And *therefore*, I act accordingly. I believe if something mentioned in the scriptures wasn't important, then it wouldn't be in the Bible. According to Mark chapter 10, Jesus was asked by the religious leaders (Pharisees) if it was right (legal) for a man to divorce his wife (the book of Matthew mentions for any cause or reason). Jesus is such a great teacher as His answers are often conveyed with a question first to get those to whom He is speaking to think. His response was, "What did Moses command you?" (Mark 10:3), asserting the authority given to Moses. They responded with Moses allowing man to give a writ (certificate) of divorcement (divorce). If you choose (that power of choice operating here) to divorce, you may.

We all have self-will so this seems agreeable, right? But this was not the original intent of God in the beginning. Man abused the law to divorce. We know divorce is not a sin, it is something that God abhors or hates and rightfully so. Man leaves his mother and father and becomes as one flesh with his wife. But why? He made woman from the rib of man, serving as a type and shadow of the unity we are to have with the Holy Spirit being in us...hence, the two shall become *one*. It's such an organic measure of nature; it was never to be desecrated. One reason is because it shows the sovereign authority given to man through the power of choice. God chooses to love us, and we choose to worship Him. We are made in His image. Therefore, we have a portion of His glory through such power; and He wants to show us this by how He honors that what we come into agreement with.

So later, Jesus' disciples asked Him the same thing the religious leaders (Pharisees) did, insinuating that they too needed clarity on the topic because they concluded it's just better not to marry (Do you see who the ultimate source for all our unknown concerns and clarity is? Yes, Him.). Jesus told them that when a man divorces his wife to marry another, he commits adultery against her and likewise for a woman. There's a principle matter here and it is seen in the measure of one's heart. People also forget that according to Matthew 5:28, Jesus expressed to the multitudes that when a man even looks upon another woman and lusts after her, he has committed adultery with her in his heart.

Remember, Jesus told the Pharisees that divorce was permitted under the law of Moses because of the hardened hearts of men, not because it was the original way. There should never be a reason for two believers who are born again in Christ to divorce. God's grace allows them to forgive one another and change. Commonly known grounds for divorce are adultery, homosexuality, bestiality, and incest.

However, divorce is not a commandment nor a requirement of the aftermath of these sins, but rather it is regulated on a permissible and limited rationale.

In 1 Corinthians chapter 7—where most debate derives from on the divorce and remarriage topic—we see the Apostle Paul speaking by way of permission unto those who are single (never married) or widowed, married (equally yoked), and married (unequally yoked). To the first group (single, never married and widows), he encouraged them to consider remaining single so they can devote themselves entirely unto the Lord. In this state, the common challenges that come with being with a spouse are spared.

As a command of the Lord, Apostle Paul said to the church regarding married individuals (equally yoked) that a woman should not separate (divorce) from her husband and if she does, she should remain single or be reconciled back to him and the husband should not leave his wife. I remember a woman of God said this to me one day (while I was separated and waiting for a confirmation on what I should do regarding my marriage under the circumstances) and although I understood the biblical reasoning behind her reference, something still didn't seem right or sit well with me concerning the matter. I was like, "Surely, I'm not bound by physical abuse to stay married to this man nor deal with infidelity." Yet I was so willing, especially if it meant I was following biblical standards as to be bound righteously to the Word. The scripture, however, serves as a premise of an individual separating or divorcing outside of the parameters of what's allowed. Reconciliation or restoration should be the first sought-after effort when divorce presents itself to the table—especially for the believers.

During the separation, I went back to my husband. I can admit I went back prematurely, out of hope and out of emotion. I was ambitious and eager to beat this demon together. He needed my help and I knew his soul was at stake. I knew who he was but what I didn't know was that he had made his choice; and out of God's sovereign nature, He honored that decision. I remember my husband shared with me a dream he had that he knew the Lord had given him. The Lord showed him two dragons with scorpion-like tails that were circling each other in the air. He said the Lord asked him two questions: "Do you lie? Do you mistreat your wife?" He responded truthfully but what the Lord implied (as he was sharing) was that if he didn't turn from his wicked ways, He would give him over to a reprobate state of mind and circle in life just as the two dragons did depicted in the vision. That was exactly what happened.

My heart goes out to victims of abuse in relationships, yet I cannot discredit the love the Father has for those who are the abusers as much as He has for those who have been victimized. Both the abuser and the abused experience the rage of demonic influences to keep them out of the will of God and from coming into the fullness of their life's purpose and destiny. When you know the right way or the right thing to do but choose not to do it, you suffer the consequences.

The other group the Apostle Paul describes are unequally yoked; and he expressed that if you marry someone who doesn't believe but chooses to dwell with you in peace, don't separate/divorce. You, being the believer, may help sanctify your spouse to become a believer of the faith. But if they want to go, let them. You are not bound to stay in that marriage because God has called us all unto peace. You probably never realized this verse, huh? We must read the Word in its entirety before assuming its implications on one's life, let alone simply allowing God to be God in their lives. My husband had a wife who was willing to stay for the sake of God's glory even though I had every reason not to. That's love.

It is so important to be whole in Christ first, so you are not swayed by the first thing that comes your way when desiring to be married. The ramifications of that decision can totally change the trajectory of your life—positively or negatively. It affects more people than just you and the person; it affects your mutual and family relationships, your children, business ventures, friendships, etc. I am grateful for the decision the Lord allowed me to make. Undesired, yes, but necessary and freeing. Nobody gets married thinking when will they get divorced. I encourage you to consider your level of wholeness before saying, "I do." So many people other than yourself will thank you for it.

"Separation"

Whew! Talk about faithfulness. She was separated from her husband for two years. She was hanging on to former prophecies she received about her marriage and family; and she knew without a shadow of a doubt that nothing was too hard for God. Nobody could tell her that what she knew to be true would indeed become a reality. She wore her ring faithfully although she made the decision during the process to separate even after that chase incident. She continued to have faith over what she knew the Lord was able to do. But what she didn't realize is that even in the waiting, two people had to come into agreement.

For those of you who are married and separated and are entertaining late night, inappropriate conversations and people, stop it! Demonstrate some temperance and control over your flesh. Engaging in this type of emotional and physical behavior is distasteful and morally wrong, especially if you are still married and intend to stay with the person from whom you are separated. You may need to set boundaries and discuss expectations of what is not acceptable if you have mutually agreed to separate. My suggestion to couples who mutually agree to separate is to seek counsel (may simply be a trusted individual/couple that provides wise advice), preferably as a couple as well as individually.

My situation was not mutual, however. I was in a predicament where my life was ultimately threatened. Let me say that domestic violence is not healthy nor should it be tolerated. It was through this experience that I understood why women stay in abusive relationships. We know domestic violence can happen from female to male, but I'll be discussing the instances from male to female. Many women stay because of hope—hope that the man will change back to the person they once knew or decided to love. That person who always made kind gestures, said the right things, and prayed together with them. The man they see now is not the man they know deep down on the inside who is displaying such out-of-control behaviors.

Many women stay because of fear—fear of being alone, being a failure, what others will think, or losing their life. It's too risky. Some women know they deserve better but hope deferred (Proverbs 13:12) still has hope without them realizing it will yet make the heart sick. Fear is crippling and will make you believe nobody cares, would understand, or is willing to help you. Many women stay because it's generational. Whoa! Who would've thought that some cycles in life are a direct result of generational curses? I've been able to identify some within my own family and let me say that if they are not dealt with at the root, then they will continue to have access to prosper in generations to come.

"The Wrong Kind of Chase"

She gets in the car with him and they begin to talk. The talk was more like her listening rather than them effectively communicating. He begins to blame her for his excess drinking and all that has happened in the marriage, including the children being taken away. She tries to get out but he locks the door. As he's pulling on her arm in a downward position, she says, "You're hurting me," as he forcibly holds her arm down with his hand. She finally gets out the car (seemingly released) and gets into the other vehicle that she was driving. She assures him she is going back home to the house. But she knew if she went back to the house, it could escalate into something much worse than where the confrontation initially began. But if she left, she didn't know where to go.

She gets to the first light and immediately turns right to try to get away from him. After following her around the city in what seems like a suspenseful thriller movie, as he repeatedly blows up her phone, she finds a way through traffic to lose him. She ends up riding around the city aimlessly, wasting gas and time, but she needed to decide what her next move was going to be. Adrenalin high, heart beating fast, and emotionally drained, she comes to a stoplight and who is miraculously across the other side of the intersection? That's right—him. She couldn't imagine after this whole time in this big metro city, how did they even run into each other again?

He follows her so she decides to pull over into a gas station. Thinking that with a lot of lights and people around, as it was getting dark at this time, he surely would not try anything stupid here. He convinces her to park the car and get in with him and leave her car parked. She gets in and he proceeds to pump some gas into the car. It was at that moment she knew this monster had grown furious and bigger than what she could handle. She came to a breaking point and it was either all or nothing in risking her life for a force that perhaps wanted her dead.

So she ran. She could feel the world moving in slow motion as her feet rose one foot after the other. Although no great sprinter, she ran into the middle of a major road towards another gas station down the way, something once again you see out of an action-packed suspense or thriller movie. "God," she says, "I need you to carry my feet." It was at that moment she felt angels on either side of her. She knew the enemy could've caught her, but he didn't even chase after her. So she runs into the local gas market. "Excuse me sir," she exclaims in shear fear for her life as she constantly keeps looking behind her waiting on her husband to come through the door. "May I use your bathroom key to lock myself in your bathroom, just for a bit?"

"Ma'am," the gas station clerk replies, "I cannot let you lock yourself in my bathroom." She noticed the clerk seemed very nonchalant about her frantic expression of fear. "Do you want me to call the police, Ma'am?" the clerk asked.

"No!" she exclaimed as she waved both her hands back and forward, although she wondered perhaps if that may be better. She didn't want to cause anything crazy to happen to him, yet she knew her life was in danger. Suddenly, she heard the gas station doorbell ring and frantically ran behind the desk of the gas station, fearing for her life as she knew it was him.

She heard the calm yet fierce anger in his voice although hidden by masked concern as he said, "Sir, I know my wife is in your store. Where is she?"

"Sir, you have to leave, or I'll call the police," the clerk said.

Wow! The police came. I had the choice to say he is doing this and doing that, but I didn't. The police officer looked me in my face and said, "Ma'am, we can't help you if you don't tell us what is going on." Many can probably relate to this or know someone who can. This is not what a wife is supposed to experience from her husband, the one who should be protecting her—yet she now needs protection from him. I didn't know what to do but I knew something needed to be done. I couldn't risk experiencing another incident like the last beat down. So I asked the officer to escort me back to the vehicle I was driving. The other officer waited with my husband to ensure he didn't follow me.

After thanking the officer and getting in the car, I headed for the interstate. Traveling northbound on I-75, I had nothing but my driver's license and $40 dollars to my name as I drove off in my father-in-law's Mustang—I know, such a savage-like moment. I had already been distanced from family/friends dealing with this narcissistic individual. It was one of the most pressing moments of my life—the quantity of such moments was increasing. **Sometimes the most intense moments of our lives are the ones we need to experience for change to happen.** This can be good or bad.

Some examples of intense moments include: accepting a job offer in another state/country, finding out your significant other cheated, hearing the lies and slander of your name/character, becoming an entrepreneur, staying, leaving, reasoning, experiencing death of a family member, being the "bigger" person, realizing you shouldn't have compromised, letting that friend go, saying yes to your gifts/talents, getting that health scare from the doctor, budget cuts at the job, and financial increase. It's those traumatic, stressful, and overwhelming (good and bad) experiences that can showcase development issues within our own character.

This was the height of what I needed to experience to help me understand what extreme resolve needed to happen, especially if God would get the glory in some miraculous way out of this situation. **Never let the actions of others dictate your value or self-worth.** It's easier said than done. Also, never judge someone for what they've done, especially if you haven't walked in their shoes or sought to understand their perspective. I'm pretty sure many of you reading this said things you would never do in life (whether good or bad) until you were tempted or the opportunity was presented to you. Let's be real!

Be the solution-finder or solution-provider in someone's life; don't add to their dismay of the challenges they are facing whether those challenges were brought on by themselves or by the actions and choices of others. Don't make them feel bad during their process, because they already do. Then after you help them, don't be that person who won't allow them to grow because you want them to need your help again because it feeds an ego of pride in your life you haven't dealt with. Know the difference between planting seeds and watering those seeds that have been planted. **Never think you are the increase-giver—that's God; let Him get that glory because it belongs to Him**.

"The Beat Down"

It was September 25, 2012. She had an interview with a real estate company in the area and was excited about this new opportunity to get into real estate as it had always been her dream. She puts on some nice heels, slacks, and a blue and white top. She leaves the house excited about the opportunity. She meets with two of the owners of the company and develops great rapport with both men. A bit intimidated initially, the interview was left with pleasant, reassuring handshakes and an invite for one more interview with the last partner of the company.

Although dreading the atmosphere of her current place of residence, she excitedly goes home to tell her husband the good news. Apparently, however, Ole Lucy had other plans—plans to derail the dream, to snatch her life away, to make her afraid to move forward towards her destiny. She scurries to grab her keys but he blocks her hand. As they tussle, with him being much bigger than her, she bends backwards as to save her face (like literally).

"I thought I told you to stay home!" her husband angrily shouts at her. Knowing how manipulation and control works hand in hand, she said nothing...thinking, 'I can't win for losing so I'll take silence as my best shot this time.' Eventually, words are exchanged, voices are elevated, and then it begins...the day only to be forgiven.

Earlier that morning, he told her, "You're not going to that interview," over the phone. He had left the house early with his father to do some labor work; and rightfully so, she had called to let him know how excited she was to get this interview and that she was getting ready to leave. Not knowing what triggered such anger and aggression, he forbids her to go, accusing her of making him look bad as a man in front of his father because she rebutted his decision. Both her and him got home and she already knew that hell was about to break loose.

Upset, tears rolling down her eyes, she's yelling, "Please, just leave me alone and let me go."

With a boisterous attitude he exclaims, "No," as he holds a smirk while looking at her attempt to move him from the door. At this point, that was nothing new to her. She was used to having her keys taken so she couldn't leave, and her phone taken so she couldn't call anybody for help. Next, his rage goes from 5 to 20. Their discord, according to her husband, was because of her. She rushes to the bathroom to flee the altercation she could feel was about to come.

He pushed in the door only to drag her out into the living space. As he pulls her to the side, he grabs a knife and proclaims how he could just kill her. Tying her neck with a scarf, then placing his hands around her neck he begins to squeeze her to the point that she is gasping for air. It was at this point she knew it could all end right here. As his hold is released, she gasps for air in over-exaggeration, hoping the whole time he would come to his senses and stop. But it doesn't stop there.

As in slow motion, she is picked up and thrown on her side on their hard tile flooring. She couldn't believe what was *happening. He does this to her about a few times and then she finds herself on the couch where he is punching her (with a soft punch) on the cheeks of her face. Not hard enough or forceful enough to leave physical bruising but enough for the emotional scars to leave soul wounds. Her eyes shut tight as she awaits the next "blow" to her jaw, knowing that it wasn't going to hurt physically but preparing for the emotional hit. His fist would touch the skin of her cheek while pressing down hard making her helpless body sink more into the couch.*

But it doesn't stop there...he gets a jug of cold water out of the refrigerator. Crying and in total amazement of how smart this demon was, he hits her with the water jug, pops the cap, and begins to pour cold water on her body. The pain she felt was so internal, she not only felt unprotected, but she also felt less than her worth. Here he was: the man she had said "yes" to, for better or for worse, for richer of for poor, in sickness and in health, until death did them part. If staying with him meant for God to get the glory, that was what she was willing to do...never thinking that God's will is not meant for us to suffer on behalf of another's wrongdoing. The aftermath left him leaving with his father (who was waiting outside for him) and her sitting there crying, only to clean the mess that he just made.

I can look back today about the fight I had with this narcissist but some battered wives/significant others cannot. Some were left for dead yet lived while others have become mere memories in the lives of the children and family they left behind. Domestic violence is no laughing matter. On average, nearly 20 people per minute are physically abused by an intimate partner in the United States. One in 4 women and 1 in 7 men have been victims of severe physical violence (beating, burning, strangling) by an intimate partner in their lifetime. One in 7 women and 1 in 18 men have been stalked by an intimate partner during their lifetime to the point where they felt very fearful or believed that they or someone close to them would be harmed or killed. Studies suggest that there is a relationship between intimate partner violence and depression and suicidal behavior (ncadv.org).

Depression and suicide surely had a reason to be welcomed in my world...my world was tumbling down. Sounds familiar? Perhaps you were the abuser in this story. Don't worry, all hope is not loss for you as I do have words of encouragement. Maybe you can connect with this story because you were her (me). You knew you were fighting something bigger than yourself and you didn't know how to defeat the giant. Well, let me share with you a few things I learned about this scene.

You see, there's this scripture that says: "We wrestle not against flesh and blood, but against principalities, against powers, against the rulers of the darkness of this world, against spiritual wickedness in high places" (Ephesians 6:12). I wasn't fighting against my husband but the spiritual entity was fighting against us. I say us because the two become one flesh once you come into covenant agreement with someone (marriage). The problem was I couldn't fight this demonic woe on my own.

We are quick to disregard the abuser as if they don't have the same color blood running through their veins. What about the spiritual/mental help they need? Who's advocating for them? God loves them too, right? Not that you must be ignorant while knowing how to interact with such individuals, but don't count them out; God is able to use them and turn them around. Pray as led and move on; that is ok to do. It's not good character to wish someone bad and speak evil words over their life or to hide unforgiveness in your heart towards them just because they caused you harm.

Consider Jesus: some people wake up every day and go to bed every night without acknowledging Him in all their ways, yet He provides and protects them. He thinks no evil thing of us so how much more should we not think evil towards others? Consider this.

"What Did You Just Say to Me?"

"I hate this place," she would utter often as she walked into the courtroom. That place made her feel uneasy. The very thought of knowing she had to be there was just wrong altogether. She would shake nervously while on the stand during trial and for various other court proceedings. The courtroom had a coldness in the air and she felt people didn't really care, they were just doing their jobs. On this final day of trial, she listens eagerly to the judge's verdict in hopes it would work out in her favor, in some miraculous way, especially since she had been praying.

She and her husband received many prophetic words concerning what God was going to do—how He was going to restore and reunify what was taken (their children). One man from up north said, "I see three children and the Lord says prepare yourselves for you are about to be reunified" and "prepare yourselves for a visitation; the Lord shall meet you." She was too excited to hear those words even when they would serve as confirmation from so many others.

However, on that day, she heard the words, "You have a mental disorder." Very stoic-like, she glazed out into the open area of the courtroom as she pondered the words recently spoken to her by the judge. She discounted it from her psyche and prevented the wickedness of the words from taking root all while feeling ashamed and embarrassed. Softly, a white sheet of paper passes between the two women sitting between her and her husband and it read, "You are a great mother." As she turned the paper over, she looked up at the judge and in her heart (as she just stared at him), asked the Lord to forgive him for speaking such negative words over her life.

The sound from the gavel hitting the mound was as piercing as a sword going through the heart of a soldier during battle. As the prosecutors and lawyers gathered documentation in relief that the three-day trial was over, she realized how commonly insignificant her life to others really seemed, especially to those just doing their job. It was at this moment that not only was her life changed forever, but she was willing to go through such a tragedy while holding on to her faith in God—the only thing she knew to trust in.

That's right, you guessed it: The verdict for the trial was given and my parental rights were taken away just like that. My husband and I decided not to voluntarily terminate our parental rights. We didn't want the kids to think we would ever choose to give them away intentionally or voluntarily, so we fought. Although the case was lost, I gained so much more in time. I couldn't see the benefits of this process then, but I understand now. I remember thinking to myself like, "Wow, how did my life get here?" Have you ever had your parental rights terminated? Do you know what that feels like? Perhaps, you know somebody who has. Well, let me enlighten you: Having your parental rights terminated is worse (to me) than knowing your child is six feet under the ground. Something buried can give closure of the loss although the grief may be acute or chronic. Knowing your children are alive and you cannot not be part of their lives, as you envisioned, hurts worse. Crazy, huh?

Better yet, have you ever gone through something in your life that you just would've never imagined you would've had to endure in a million years? What in the world just happened to me? Why was this happening? I sometimes don't even know how I even pulled it all together. I can only thank God for resiliency. Back in 2010, I started my master's program in mental health counseling. Can you imagine the humiliation and embarrassment I must've felt (me of all people) to be told I had a mental disorder? After the trial, I had gone into a sunken place. I battled with suicidal thoughts often and of course, the infamous *depression*. I remember driving down a hill on 39th Avenue thinking how quick and not too painful it would be if I just smashed the vehicle into a tree in the median—but God.

I had a little less than a year to finish the mental health counseling program (while maintaining a 3.0 GPA) in which I was enrolled; but due to the pain of now knowing the trial was over and my parental rights were taken away, I just gave up. The outcome was not what I was anticipating. I look back and thank God, however, for intervening the way He did. My family was about to self-destruct and before a major tragedy could've taken place (a freak accident or even death), God allowed a different route. More importantly, He knew I had the capacity to deal with the hurt of it all and be stretched to develop and grow from it in the process.

Have you ever had that one life-changing moment to which you can attribute much of your growth to experiencing what Ole Lucy meant for bad? Maybe you had a soul tie with someone so strong you thought you would truly never get over the breakup. Perhaps you needed a financial miracle like yesterday or that one time and thought if something didn't pull through you were just going to die...but you are still here. Maybe you were the person who had to result sleeping in a shelter with your children/family for a season or that family that lost everything in a house fire. Maybe you were that woman whose auto accident caused low self-esteem because of the scars it left on your face. Maybe you were the person whose doctor said that you would never walk again or the individual whose parent just passed away and that was the only person who you felt had your back. Maybe you were that faithful guy who was cheated on by a woman you gave your whole heart to. Maybe you were the person who had to experience long-term infirmities due to an accident or adverse health risks. Maybe you were touched inappropriately by someone who was supposed to protect you. Maybe you were that little girl or little boy who was raped and still need to go through a healing process. I know I've mentioned some of these before but to emphasize, we've all had intense circumstances that are what I call "death" experiences.

One of the most important things to remember when going through a process in your own life is to not allow the words of others to dictate your destiny, not allow your thoughts to make you forget who you are (and Whose you are), and not forget that what you suffer through is not worth comparing to the victory you already have and the blessings you will receive for overcoming. You were born strong and whatever you had to endure that was/is not common to most and misunderstood by many, know that there is purpose even in your strength.

"Have you considered my servant Job?" Do you remember this quote? From what book? Yes, the Bible (Job 1:8, NIV). Ole Lucy was doing what he was supposed to since getting thrown out of Heaven…seeking whom he may devour (1 Peter 5:8). Literally, God tells him to try (to devour, steal, kill, destroy) Job. I know, it sounds like God low-key threw Job under the bus, right? We know He is a just God. It wouldn't be a fair fight to simply annihilate the enemy, because we know that God can easily do this all by

Himself (I mean, He is the Creator of Ole Lucy). So out of His sovereign will, God allows Ole Lucy access to mess with things in Job's life (cattle, possessions, livelihood, children, etc.) and to destroy it to showcase that He will still get the glory out of man's life. This is how we know that battles we fight in life are not our own. Through the redemptive Blood of Jesus, we can be vessels for God's glory.

"My Little Amigos"

The hour is late and with every tick and every tock, reality starts to gravitate to her heart even more. She was going home but not with her babies. The children she birthed into the world—with her first being 8lbs 15oz (technically a 9lb baby) and the youngest (at the time)—would be in the hands of complete strangers. This woman knew how to hide her hurt very well. Knowing the nurses/doctors were staring as she walked out of that hospital room, she agreeably grabs her husband's hand and walks out the door.

Silent on the ride home, her world crumbled inside. Unimaginably, the notion of knowing that DCF would be part of her history in a way she would've never imagined in all her life didn't hit her until she walked through the door of her apartment. Collapsed on the bare floor, her body wreaks a pain never known to a human—that she knew of at least— and she cried enough tears in a night to fill the Jordan River. She wept and cried and wept and cried. Her husband cried too. Her world turned from gray to pitch black all in a matter of hours.

September 2011 was the beginning of the year that would change her life forever—for worse first and then for better. Amazingly, she would yet have faith and build her trust in the Lord.

Out of all people, would I begin to feel such heartache. I remember that day like it was yesterday…man, the emotional pressure I felt. For so long it was just my daughter and me. I was a full-time single parent who lived on public housing, worked a full-time job, and was a full-time student at the University of Florida. I look back sometimes and wonder how I was even doing that. A mother has an abnormal amount of strength when it comes to her children. I didn't have time for excuses, I just had to be mommy. I remember those days like they were yesterday. I had my daughter in my junior year of college. I took a year off because I didn't like the idea of sending her to daycare so young around people I didn't know…plus I didn't want to spend too much time away from her either.

Going to college was seemingly just one of those non-negotiable things in life. I had always been resilient so this too would make no difference. I got back enrolled and finished my degree. Upon getting married not long after graduation, I had my son a year later. These precious babies were my heart. I thought I had married someone who loved my daughter as his own...yet I would be sadly mistaken later on. Never would I have thought that my children would've been ripped away from me all because of the person I chose to marry and chose to love. But thank God that in my weakness, He is strong so that I may endure the process that pushed me into destiny.

I don't believe you have to experience something to be expert on it; however, there's a conviction that comes from the ones who have. I have compassion for families that deal with issues involving the State. I have a passion for children not with their parents, especially parents who care. I can sympathize with those who have been the victim at the hands of another. I believe in restoration of families and have a heart for those who were/are the victimizer/abuser. I cannot afford for my heart to be filled with bitterness, anger, and hurt from that type of pain. **Pain has a powerful way it**

produces the pressure needed to promote and push you into your promise and purpose. So, let pain propel you to that place—your expected end after the storm.

"And Scene"

People you connect with can either change the whole trajectory of your life, whether it be delay of rightful momentum for moving forward or a sudden catapult into destiny and purpose. Many times, certain people in our lives—like haters—are necessary to propel us to our place of destiny. While this is true, much of our *chosen* connections have to do with where we are and where we should be at a point and time in life. We should always evaluate if the people in our lives are helping us fulfill purpose or serving as a hindering factor. Some bad connections are necessary to be aware of the need to refocus.

Your experiences of life—whether good or bad—have a direct link to who you are connected to, typically by choice, outside of the family you were born into. For example, a "good kid" hanging with his/her peers who perform reckless and ruthless behavioral acts can suffer the same consequences legally. On the flip side, you can have a business and decide to partner with someone who sees the vision and simply wants to partake and be part of what you are doing without ulterior motives. You don't have to allow toxic people to ruin seasons in your life and derail or delay your destiny. Get to know people, observe the fruit that they bear and most importantly, ask God for discernment to show you the things you can't see.

PART THREE

"Much prayer and much fasting will be required of you two," were the words spoken to them by one of the ladies of their church. They were married for about five years. Thankfully, someone knew what it was going to take for that marriage to work. In the beginning of their marriage, things were great. Both knew they shared that desire to be loved by a significant other and with the individual call of God on their lives, they knew the term "power couple" was inevitable.

"What did you dream about?" her husband would ask often.

"I had a dream that we were both running in this town which later turned into a field and..."

"Wait!" he says excited to know he too had a similar dream. "Was there a yellow truck?"

With that 'OMG, get out of here look,' she candidly expresses, "Yes!"

This becomes all too common as they both continued to grow and learn of each other. Several times, they would finish each other's dreams; what a connection they had. The enemy too knew the connection was strong enough to dethrone his demonic plans and thus, would do all he was given the power to do to deter the words 'power' and 'couple' from ever being used by them.

When two people walk in agreement, it's powerful. You see, she was a strong person and could wear her hurt on her shoulders so well it looked invisible with her smile— especially to those who had no keen sense of discernment or intuition. The abuse had started with words that eventually led into verbal abuse. That's how it always begins...with words spoken in the atmosphere.

Not understanding then what she knows now about dream interpretation, the snippet of that dream was to serve as caution. Fields can represent spiritual warfare or a battlefield while a yellow (caution) and truck (ministry type) can represent something to be aware of or to consider or a forewarning. Something was shifting or happening. Around this season of her life, the blue skies were starting to turn dim. The day was at the brink of darkness and unexpectedly fiery darts pierce her in her chest as her knees buckle down to the ground (she doesn't die though). She can see the many faces of fear—situations and circumstances—inching closer towards her as a lion does its prey. While she weeps, her silent screams are as loud as a tree falling in the forest even though nobody is around. In some supernatural way, she manages to get up and begins to drag herself to safety—to the house on a hill far from the field only to find out the home on the hill was as dark inside as the battlefield was outside. Resilient to see the light, she pulls herself up by the bootstraps and declares, "This too shall pass." She didn't know that it was just the beginning.

The beginning of something seems so hard at first sometimes. Have you ever started a business and in the beginning, your sales seemed a bit bleak? What about having those systems and processes in place, though (ugh)? Maybe you realized like, "Whoa, entrepreneurship is not all what it's cracked up to be." You thought things were going to be easy, but you literally had to put in some major sweat equity in the business. I get it; it's work. Perhaps you walked into a drought season in your life—regarding your money, relationships, job, health, etc.—and it started to have this downward spiral only to be topped off with the length of time you've had to endure it.

My days, although good on the outside, were indeed growing darker from within. Nobody wants their family to dislike the person they've chosen to love. Sometimes, it can seem hard to love someone your family doesn't like. Maybe you've experienced the infamous conversations about "whose side of the family are we spending the holidays with this year" or "your parents don't even like me" or "I can't stand your siblings." This is where some true solid foundational barriers will need to be enforced and/or established. Sure, I loved this person. I can admit, I may have been out of this person's league (initial thoughts) although I gave him no reason to feel as such. Yeah, I noticed a few red flags about his character, but this guy had potential. In fact, many days while I was emotionally detached from my husband, I would commit to my "wifely duties" of having marital sex out of wanting to honor God's Word. My body no longer was my own but became as one with whom I said, "I do."

I knew how to love but being in love was short-lived in the marriage. There was no reciprocity there—no liberation for me to—just be—me. I had an understanding that the enemy had an ingenious way of sowing tares in the minds of man to make them feel as if they had the equitable right to seek out other forms of sinful nature and make it justifiable. I surely didn't want to be the provocation of such behavior. But I told you that I married potential: that's where I messed up at. He was jovial in nature, very charming, and most importantly, treated my daughter with what I deemed as any caring parent would at the time. I learned to just smile many days early in the relationship, perhaps assuming it all just comes with the territory of marriage. Those red flags began to show even more stronger and then I knew something was off here, but I only focused on the good.

Focusing only on the good and never considering the bad makes it hard to cope when the bad arises. Growing up, many times you are taught (non-verbally) that what happens in your home stays in your home. It's usually not until something happens that you seem to have no choice but to talk then. But that too is a problem. Those who can see red flags should definitely say something. Saying something doesn't mean you spread their business, but you know how to provide wisdom and a resolve to their problem with integrity to such personal matters. A word in due season—how great is it (Proverbs 15:23). Many people can see someone falling, choose not to say anything, but express, "I knew it," when something major or openly happens. I pray God gives you the grace, tact, wisdom, and understanding to expose, express, and reveal—to a friend or loved one without judgment or condemnation—what they need to hear or do to help them with making better choices.

Each day of added darkness—although not desired—was shaping my character, my stamina was increasing, and resiliency gained a new measure and meaning to my life. I didn't realize it at first because it didn't seem fair. I was a good wife, submissive, and willing to follow my husband even though it caused me to be isolated from family, eventually friends, and ultimately myself. Today, even more, have I been appreciative of this situation. It has exposed generational curses in my bloodline that were dormant or unknown. I've learned to count it all joy (James 1:2) and embrace the season for what it was…or is. It was developing me into the woman I have grown to be today, and the best is yet to come.

"The Orange and Blue"

She was headed to the University of Florida. You couldn't tell her nothin'. She graduated in the Top 6% of her high school class and was relieved once she got that acceptance letter in the mail. Attending UF as an African American student wasn't as peachy as she thought it was going to be though. For one, she felt the sting of attending a predominately Caucasian, flagship university. She walked from McCarty Hall C one day thinking, "Will this experience feel fun or different soon?"

She purposely got involved with organizations to defer the sense of not belonging. She participated in organizations such as the Black Student Union, the Florida Invitational Step Show (FISS), University Gospel Choir, FYCS club, etc. Although she easily met acquaintances and made friends, the lack of inclusivity could still be felt on campus. She was never one to party and can count on one hand how many times she went to the club.

The other "not so peachy" part was the only thing holding you accountable was personal drive and the grades posting on your Blackboard or student portal. Raise her hand? You mean to tell her she could just get up without a word and leave the classroom without being stopped or questioned where she was going? You mean to tell her she could choose not to even show up for class? So on the real, she really loved school—well, really, really, liked school. She was one of those grade school kids who cried and asked "why" if she had to be taken out of school for a dental appointment, etc. Yes, she was that girl.

College was fun and freeing. But with the many freedoms that come with college, there were also consequences when those freedoms are abused. For the most part, she was in class all of the time. It's during this time in a person's life that they are learning about themselves and forever changing. It is also during these times that some of the stupidest mistakes are made whether influenced by fear, social norms, and/or peer pressure.

Like an idiot, UF was the only college I applied to—which I encourage you youngsters NOT to do—and by the grace of God, I got in. I remember what I felt like on this big campus coming straight from high school. I was excited yet overwhelmed—Not in a bad way though, but a challenge rather. I grew up as a military kid and we traveled a lot for most of my young life so adapting to new environments were not problematic for me. I knew college was inevitable so it was a no-brainer that I was going right after high school. It was during this time or season of my life that I found out more and more about myself.

I drove a blue 1989 Oldsmobile Cutlass Sierra. Mr. Blue was his name (raise your hand if you too name your cars). My friends would call it "old and busted," yet they had no problem riding in it; that, or they were just using me by allowing me to call them friend. I was that friend who took my friends to the grocery store because buying groceries while using the city transit system (the bus) can suck. Many days, it felt like I peed on myself every time I got to campus driving that car. I commuted 30 minutes every day to campus and my windows were not tinted, so the sun had this disrespectful way of beaming through the windows and heating up every moral fiber of my body.

Initially, I was adapting well regarding being successful during my college experience. I eventually got involved with a guy who was a "dope boy" (someone who distributes illicit substances). It was during this relationship that I found out how naïve I really was. I signed a lease in my name for this guy only to be evicted three months later (yep and it didn't come off my credit report until seven years later, legit); risked losing my scholarships and affordability of being a UF student being at the trap house (a place where illegal drugs are sold); and experienced my first heartbreak of being cheated on, which left me to experience the roller coaster ride of retrieving sexually transmitted diseases and emotional upheaval.

The best thing from that relationship, however, is my daughter. I learned a lot from that experience. It is one of the reasons I feel passionate today about the importance of the validation children should feel at home while they are young and growing into that place of young adulthood. Teaching young people self-efficacy, self-worth, and emotional maturity are extremely important in how they fair along as young adults with decision making...especially with relationships. This does not go against my mother's or father's upbringing efforts and parenting skills, but I wish I would have been exposed and expressed more about the things to consider when engaging in romantic relationships. I witnessed much that I shouldn't have growing up and it definitely played a role in my personal experiences as a young adult.

In high school, I remember saying how college was supposed to be my time to showcase who God was, how fun-loving the Lord can be for young adults. I was supposed to be radical and on fire for Christ, yet I found myself walking in a sinful life that brought about personal shame upon myself. I smoked a few Black & Milds (never had weed or cigarettes), had a few alcoholic beverages (never experienced a hangover) and yes, I fornicated. I know, stop gasping for breath and close your mouth; we all have things in our past we aren't happy about. Much of that lifestyle didn't happen until I met ole dope boy. Nevertheless, we have the power to make right choices and not allow the choices of others to persuade us to do what we know we shouldn't be doing in the first place. Therefore, choose your company wisely. The company you keep reflects who you are—it's reflective in your character, the way you think, your behavior, and your decisions. He had become the company I kept and my actions manifested as such. I knew we were on very different paths spiritually and were not equally yoked.

Multiple times throughout my college experience, I found myself remorseful over choices I had made and would find myself repenting of my sinful nature. You may know what this feels like. In fact, most people who are called and chosen by God to do a great work can't just sin and not feel bad about it or convicted by (the) Holy Spirit. There are people who sin all the time without regard to the spiritual implications of the consequences their sins bring into their life. They keep indulging in sin because of the instant pleasure and satisfaction it brings, even if it shows a negative connotation about their character. Deliverance is available to us all; we just have to want it bad enough to stop our sinful ways.

"Cow Patty High"

There she was walking the field at North Marion High School (best known as "Cow Patty High") looking at family who came from afar to congratulate her on the journey as a new high school graduate. It was May 2003 and she couldn't have been happier. She walked across the stage many times to receive several awards at the ceremony the night before. All the hard work over the course of the last four years had paid off. Her classes, except some elective courses, were high honors, advanced placement (AP), and dual enrollment (college courses). She was part of the minority in these classes although the school had a diverse population. You would think the race disparity at the University of Florida was all too normal for her—it was for the most part. She circled the same group of other African American students who were also in advanced courses.

She never got in a fight, sent to detention, or had any major disciplinary actions—high school seemed like a breeze. Her "friends" knew that with her upbringing, there was a limit to the type and amount of extracurricular activities she was able to partake in. She ran track (she was that 3rd heat slow), was in student government, played the clarinet in band for a bit, and participated in a few other after-school activities.

You could find her for the most part in Mrs. Jacqueline Gary's (the guidance counselor) office during lunch filling out scholarships for college, especially during her senior year. She probably applied for 13 or more scholarships but only received 6. She was that girl who would be cool enough with others that she got invited to stuff but everyone knew she wouldn't come, predominately because she wouldn't be allowed. However, this one time, she was invited to a birthday party and could go, but only for a few hours. The friend whose birthday it was received a "lap dance" and it made her feel uncomfortable. She felt out of place.

"Aren't you going to dance?" they would ask as she would shy away, just sitting and shaking her head "no." It was in one of those moments that she knew she was different than the majority. She promised herself that she would relentlessly live the life of a young person who loved the Lord radically and wouldn't be ashamed to let the world know.

You ever have a time frame that you'd go back to in life knowing what you know now? I'd probably go to the end of high school. I can remember the pungent yet inviting smell of cow manure (hence the school nickname) stepping off the bus. High school was fun. It's that time you get to make some long-lasting friendships—some perhaps for a lifetime—as you emerge into the young-adult life. It can also be dark and gloomy for a lot of students. Physical changes, changes within the family dynamics, bullying, inconsistent grades, etc. can all be derived from external environmental factors outside the classroom. Parental guidance may be nonexistent in the home or "over-existent."

I remember having to work with my stepdad for his lawn care service. I was used to going to visit my biological dad and family in Mississippi—both my brother and I. So to start helping with the business—well, I hated it. Waking up at 5am everyday over the summer, getting in late, and freezing water the night before to have cold water for the day sucked as a teenager. I was young when my summers started with laborious work. However, I learned a great trade although it was hard work indeed. I would have these big clear goggles on to cover my eyes from debris. You may have caught me wearing a green, long sleeve turtleneck—I know, in the dead of summer—with some long pants and a hat. I was not trying to turn a thousand different shades before the school year would start back again.

There were times when I would be left at a house to complete a job alone. This one time, I was left at a local restaurant (off a major highway) with a bed of flowers and told to make the landscape look pretty and that it needed to be done by the time my stepdad came back. Oh, the pressure! From trimming hedges, weed-eating and using Round-Up to using/pushing a leaf blower and an edge trimmer…you name it, I'd done it all by the tender age of 13.

Although I had calloused hands, it taught me good work ethics and I've grown to be very appreciative of the experience. I also had to clean the whole house from top to bottom and if I missed wiping down a window sill or taking the garbage out, then I didn't clean the house at all. We traveled on vacations here and there and for the most part, I can honestly say that I had a decent childhood. However, there were some things that I wish I didn't experience or witness during that time as well.

"Generational Things"

"Stop!" her mom would yell. She was outside washing the vehicles, one of her typical chores she did over the weekends. Heart beating fast with every moment of a screech she would hear, praying nothing "crazy" was going on inside. "Ahhhhh!" she heard the fear in her mother's voice that time.

The water hose flies out of her hand, slightly spraying her in the face as she curbs the vehicle jumping over the bucket of water and soap as fear and adrenalin has frightened her about what could happen next...all while angry. Boom! The back door slams. Hoping it would bring a halt to the altercation going on inside between her mom and step-dad, within seconds, the heat was turned on her.

"Don't you slam my door no more," her stepdad would angrily say while pointing his finger at her.

"Don't hit my mama," she would respond with an angry expression on her face that could kill.

Suddenly there was this tightening around her neck, growing more and more intense. Her step-dad was choking her. She had this fierce look in her eyes where he knew whatever he was doing to her, it couldn't amount to the pain she felt seeing her mom being hurt by the man who was at least supposed to protect her. She couldn't remember how it all even ended that night or how the next days had come and gone, but this wasn't the first time she remembered something like that.

When she was much younger, she remembered running up the stairs with her mom and brother away from their biological dad, her mom's first husband. Her dad was banging on the door and to try to protect her and her brother, her mom went out the room. She and her brother would sit on the bed holding each other crying as they listened to the arguing and sounds of violence. Yet again, days would come as if nothing happened prior. The unconditional love of a child knows no division—division is fed through the words of a hurt adult to the mind of a child.

I have few vivid memories as a kid growing up where my biological dad and mom had some physical altercations. The psychological effects of physical, verbal, mental, or sexual abuse can negatively impact a person's life for an extended period—even generations after. As a matter of fact, I have come to realize that my experience with it has been a direct result of a generational curse. Both my parents have been married and divorced twice. Now my brother and I have both been married and divorced once. My mother was a victim of physical abuse in both of those marriages and now I too had my experience. I will never ask a woman why she stays. I get it. And why many may pass judgment about what they would never do...never say what you wouldn't do until you have been put in that situation.

Being a victim of undue influence or duress takes a toll on a person's mental and physical ability to overcome or persevere. Control and manipulation are real. There's that hope that things would get better because of the truth of knowing that's not who that person really is. **Reality and hope are different things and it's important to know *when* to take the two off of the same path.**

"And Scene"

Family matters and no man is an island; therefore, you can't grow alone. Whew! We can go into many conversations on that statement alone. Specifically, family serves as the building block of how we interact with the world around us. The composition of family may be displayed as two married individuals, parenthood and of course, extended members of the family lineage. Family helps set the tone of the life its members most likely will live whether the experience is positive or negative. A male child may have experienced growing up without a father for example. That doesn't mean he won't be an active participant father in his child's life. If a family member can only talk about another without resolve of helping that individual, then they are part of the problem; this is so common among families.

I advocate for family restoration and believe there is nothing so hurtful a family member has done that can't be forgiven and time redeemed for the restoration of that relationship. There are societal standards and common expectations of what family members are "supposed" to do and not do. A father is supposed to lead, protect, and provide for their children...true. Fathers have also been known to be sexually and physically abusive to their children, leaving boys and girls not knowing how to cope with issues of abandonment and rejection and causing them to indulge in identity crisis. A mother should be there to nurture and help train her children up in the way they should go (Proverbs 22:6)…true. Mothers have also been known to be jealous of and manipulative with their children because of the lack of validation and liberation as a woman they experienced, leaving boys and girls not knowing how to be expressive in their emotions and leaving room for timidity and fear to thrive. So, family does matter. If it was not true, it would not be reflective of the impact that a family leaves on every dimension of our well-being: social, physical, emotional, intellectual, spiritual, economical, etc.

Many today, for whatever reason, have not always revered their family as *family*. Perhaps the family was responsible for something that caused them public shame. While we cannot pick our families, we can choose how we interact and respond to our family. While family is extremely important to one's life, the other most significant family connection is spiritual. Your spiritual family is not bound by ethnicity, gender, or social standing. Scripture tells us, according to Matthew 12:50, that whoever does the will of the Father which is in Heaven, is more family to me than blood relatives. Your spiritual family are those who are like-minded and support your efforts of bringing the Kingdom into the earth.

Wow! These scenes were just snippets of my life yet so meaningful. First, let me express to you how hard it is to remain humble during this process I've experienced. It takes strength in character and a toughness to endure the notion of what people think they know about you but actually have no idea. The process of going through something because of what another person has caused or did seems to be unfair many times, especially considering the things you've had to sacrifice because of it. Maybe that looks like giving up people, places, and things.

Remember, a process is a series of events or steps that get you from where you are to where you should, desire to, or will be over a given time period. Sometimes you'll go through things in life because God knew He could trust you with the weight that came with it. You see, the war you fight in life is not only a battle that has already been won (a finished work), it's a fight of your faith and simply believing what God said you already have authority over. I've had to fight many days on my knees. In fact, since a teenager, I would cry out to the Lord in silence in my closet. I'd lock myself away in my room, go in my closet (I know, I took the scripture literally here), and talk to the Lord…usually ending with tears and snot rolling down my face.

Most believe in the coined phrase, "trust the process." Meaning, things look a little bleak right now but you know it's going to get better. I've told my children many days "it won't be like this always" and to know that the process has to run its course the way God intended. Your process won't look like another's and it won't always look like what you want it to. But we must believe by faith that everything that seems bad now will work out even when it doesn't look like it will. It's faith. According to scripture, "Now faith is the substance of things hoped for, the evidence of things not seen" (Hebrews 11:1). It took faith to write this book and share parts of my story, and it's going to take faith to believe that it will impact someone in a positive way.

I attribute my resiliency through all of this to God. There are three reasons why I believe I have experienced the things I have in my life thus far (maybe you can relate): First, there are things we go through in life because God has chosen us to experience it, not because of something bad we have done. I think about the story of Job in the Bible. Like Job, God can trust many today to showcase His glory. Through trials and tribulations, God allows His glory to shine through our obedience, consistency, diligence, discipline, and servitude unto Him as victory against demonic powers.

Second, there are things we go through in life because of the things that another has done (or not done) before us: parents, generational curses, bloodline, ancestors, etc. Sometimes children experience the consequences of the iniquities of their forefathers who have gone on before them but did not have the knowledge (or did not know how to apply what they did know) to sever those curses at their roots. I implore you to break generational curses so that your children don't have to deal with them. The Bible says that "A good man leaves an inheritance to his children's children" (Proverbs 13:22). Inheritance does not just pertain to financial wealth but also spiritual implications of living life in its abundance—the way God intended.

Third, there are things we go through in life because of things *we* have done (or not done). Our own personal choices will be reflective of what we experience in life. If poor decisions are made, you'll reap the consequences as such. If good decisions are made, you'll reap the consequences as such. Life is about choices. Those choices will dictate your processes most times. Even if you are chosen to experience great exhausting circumstances, you can choose the way you respond during that time so that it may be more bearable while going through it.

What process(es) have you experienced in life, good or bad, that have attributed to your growth? When's the last time you were grateful for the experience? Who's the last person you shared your story with? We overcome in life by the word of our testimony (Revelation 12:11). Share what you desire about your life to those who need to hear it—It's your story. Own it. Grow through it as you go through it. Learn from it, then teach others.

Your process may look different than mine. It may be better or worse. It may be longer or shorter. It may be simple or tragic. It's your story and most definitely your process. Never let anyone minimize your processed moments of life. Everyone's destiny is different along this path called life but ultimately, we have the same purpose: to be impactful to those whom we meet along the way, showcasing the Father's love, forgiveness, and glory in *the process*. I pray you have been blessed by my story.

Author Bio

Chantelle Smith has taken on the world of becoming a self-published author. Born as a "military kid" in Germany, she affords much of her resiliency to her ability to adapt to constant change from her experiences relocating throughout the states growing up. After settling in Florida for most of her young adult life, she obtained her Bachelor's degree in Family, Youth, and Community Science with a minor in Leadership from the University of Florida (2009) and her Master's degree in Business Administration from Saint Leo University (2016). Licensed as a Realtor since 2016, she has served on the Young Professionals Network and the Global International Real Estate Council committees. She is the proud Owner/Founder of The Expectancy Institute, LLC, which is a consulting agency whose mission is to provide practical leadership training to businesses and personal development services for individuals. She additionally serves as the Executive Director of MOTIV8U of North Central Florida, Inc., which is a non-profit organization that provides inspirational and engaging training programs to public and private partners with a focus geared towards the youth—guiding them to understand their personal value and the value of others. Her Christian faith affords her the opportunity to help individuals hone the focus on the change needed in both their professional and personal endeavors. She believes her life is ministry and therefore, she does not separate the two. She enjoys meeting new people, traveling, serving others, a good laugh, great food, and most importantly, her family—all while living to experience life in its abundance.

www.theexpectancyinstitute.com

www.facebook.com/theexpectancyinstitute

www.instagram.com/theexpectancyinstitute